# SU...
# COUNTRY RECIPES

### COMPILED BY
### MOLLY PERHAM

### RAVETTE BOOKS

Published by Ravette Books Limited
3 Glenside Estate, Star Road
Partridge Green, Horsham,
Sussex RH13 8RA
(0403) 710392

Production: Oval Projects Ltd.
Cover design: Jim Wire
Typesetting: Repro-type
Printing & binding: Nørhaven A/S

All recipes are given in Imperial and Metric
weights and measures. Where measurements
are given in 'cups', these are American cups,
holding 8 fluid ounces.

The recipes contained in this book are traditional
and many have been compiled from archival sources.
Every effort has been made to ensure that the recipes
are correct.

Acknowledgements:
Grateful thanks to Mrs. R. Gitsham of Trimley St. Martin, nr.
Ipswich, for Suffolk Rusks (another way).

# RECIPES

# SUFFOLK

The county of Suffolk consists of gently undulating countryside with a coastline of low cliffs and dunes, intersected by the mouths of rivers. The quiet charm of the landscape has been the inspiration of two great English artists — Gainsborough and Constable.

Suffolk has ideal agricultural land. Wheat has long been one of the main crops, so that recipes using flour such as dumplings, puddings and pies, are a major part of the staple diet. Many festive dishes are connected with the growing of wheat: Seed Cake celebrated the completion of the sowing; Fourses Cake the harvesting. The grainfields attract all sorts of game. Shooting parties used to be popular on the large estates and the countryman was able to fill the cooking-pot with a rabbit or hare when meat was scarce.

The land and climate are suitable for all kinds of vegetables and fruit — peas, beans, spinach, root vegetables, strawberries, raspberries, gooseberries and plums all flourish here.

Suffolk's long coastline provides plenty of fish, including whiting, cod, plaice and sole. Shellfish are gathered on the mudflats, using buckets, nets, spears and rakes. From the fish huts on the beaches at Southwold, Dunwich and Aldeburgh the local catch can be bought fresh each day. The herring industry has been centred on Lowestoft since medieval times, but it no longer has the same importance in the 20th century. During its heyday, the catches were so great that fisher-girls used to come down from Scotland for the season to gut the herring and pack them in barrels, well-salted to preserve them on their long journey to northern Europe. There was also a trade in bloaters and kippers, and some of the curing sheds can still be seen. The sea and the rivers provided a gateway for trade with the Continent.

In the marshy creeks and dykes along the river mouths men still go out at night to catch eels with nets and traps. Sheep used to graze on the marshes, almost at the water's edge, eating the wild samphire that can still be found in certain places. Suffolk sheep are a cross between the Norfolk horned breed and the black-faced Southdown, and provide good quality mutton.

Suffolk has been noted for its dairy cattle, too, the Suffolk Dun having a long history and yielding a large quantity of milk. Butter made from the milk was much praised by William Camden in the 17th century: 'For quantity and quality this county doth excel... the child not yet come to and the old man who is past the use of teeth, eateth no softer, the poor man no cheaper, the rich man no wholesomer food...'

The same cannot be said of Suffolk cheese, which is very hard as it is made with skimmed milk. A story is told that a parcel of Suffolk cheese was packed in an iron chest and put on board a ship bound for the West Indies. The rats, attracted by the smell, gnawed a hole in the chest, but could not penetrate the cheese.

The pig was a staple item in the diet, and most families kept one in a sty at the end of the garden. It was an easy animal to rear and feed, and the flesh was suitable for preserving, so that there was a supply of meat that would last throughout the year. After the autum pig-killing the carcase was laid on a pig-bench and the backbone, or chine, was cut out. Then the skin was singed to get rid of the hair, and the carcase hung up until it was wanted for cutting. Nothing from the pig was wasted. The offal was eaten up first as pig's fry, or turned into sausages and brawn. Hams were cured and hung up to dry for the winter months ahead.

The country cottage used to have a brick oven built into the wall of the kitchen. This was heated by burning faggots of hedge-cuttings or furze. When the required temperature was reached, the embers were removed and the day's baking was put inside — cakes, pies and tarts at the back, followed by meat pies and sausages, milk pudding and bread. The embers were taken over to the hearth and used to heat a cauldron of water suspended on a hook, in readiness for the washing up.

Suffolk is a unique mixture of land and sea, and the traditional foods of the county reflect the link between the two in some strange combinations, such as herrings with dumplings. In days gone by men worked on the land harvesting the wheat, and then moved to the coast to harvest the herring.

'And so home, where I found my wife vexed at her people for grumbling to eat Suffolk Cheese which I am also vexed at, and so to bed.'

Samuel Pepys from his *Diary* — 4th October 1661

# PARSNIP AND APPLE SOUP          Serves 4-6

Suffolk is a good place for growing root vegetables — parsnips, carrots and turnips — which are ideal for making nourishing winter soup.

**1½ lbs (675 g) parsnips**
**1 cooking apple**
**2 oz (50 g) butter**
**2 pints (1 litre/5 cups) stock**
**5 sage leaves**
**¼ pint (150ml/⅔ cup) cream**
**Salt and pepper**
**1 tablespoon chopped parsley**

Peel and dice the parsnips.

Peel, core and slice the apple.

Melt the butter in a heavy saucepan and cook the parsnip and apple gently over a low heat for 5 minutes, until soft.

Add the stock and sage leaves.

Bring to the boil, cover, and simmer for about 30 minutes, or until the parsnip is really tender.

Remove the sage leaves and blend the soup in a liquidizer, or pass through a sieve.

Return the soup to the pan, add the cream, and season to taste.

Re-heat before serving, taking care not to allow it to boil once the cream is added, and sprinkle with chopped parsley.

# VEGETABLE WATER SOUP     Serves about 6

**A quarter of a cabbage**
**4 carrots**
**2 parsnips**
**3 turnips**
**6 onions**
**1 celery root**
**A small parsley root**
**A few leaves of chervil**
**½ pint (300 ml/1¼ cups) peas, tied in a muslin bag**
**2 pints (1.15 litres/5 cups) water**
**Salt**

Wash the vegetables well but do not cut them up.

Put them in a large saucepan and cover with 2 pints (1.15 litres/5 cups) water.

Bring to the boil and simmer for 3 hours.

Strain off the liquid and return it to the saucepan.

Season with salt.

Cut up some of the vegetables into dice to garnish the soup.

Re-heat before serving.

# SPRING SOUP

Serves 4-6

1 pint (600 ml/2½ cups) green peas
A few lettuce leaves
A handful of herbs — chervil, purslain, sorrel, parsley, etc.
3 onions
1 oz (25 g) butter
Warm water
3 egg yolks
¼ pint (150 ml/⅔ cup) milk
Salt and pepper

Melt the butter in a large saucepan, and add the peas, chopped herbs and sliced onions.

Shake over the heat for a few minutes.

Add the same proportion of warm water.

Bring to the boil and simmer until all the vegetables and herbs are soft.

Strain off the liquid and pass the vegetables through a sieve.

Heat the vegetable pulp with three parts of the liquid.

Mix the remaining part with the egg yolks and milk.

Stir this into the rest of the soup and heat until it thickens.

Season to taste.

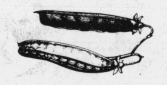

# SUFFOLK SPINACH SOUP WITH DUMPLINGS

Serves 4

1 lb (450 g) spinach
1 onion
1 carrot
1 stick celery
1 sprig each of parsley and thyme
1 oz (25 g) uncooked rice
1½ pints (900 ml/ 3¾ cups) stock
A knob of butter
Salt and pepper

For the dumplings:
4 oz (100 g) self-raising flour
2 oz (50 g) shredded suet
A pinch of salt
Water

Wash and finely shred the vegetables and herbs.

Put into a saucepan with the rice and stock.

Bring to the boil and simmer for 30 minutes.

Blend all the cooked ingredients in a liquidizer, or pass through a sieve.

Return to the pan, add a knob of butter and season to taste.

**To make the dumplings:**

Mix together the flour, shredded suet and salt.

Add enough water to bind the ingredients together.

Shape the dough into 8 small balls.

Bring the soup back to the boil, drop in the drumplings and simmer for a further 15 minutes.

# SUFFOLK DUMPLINGS (another way)

**1 lb (450 g) plain flour**
**A pinch of salt**
**½ oz (15 g) lard**
**½ oz (15 g) fresh yeast**
**1 level teaspoon sugar**
**Warm milk**

Sift the flour and salt into a mixing basin.

Rub in the lard.

Cream the yeast with the sugar and a little warm milk.

Pour this into the flour and add enough warm milk to make an elastic dough.

Knead well until the dough is smooth.

Cover the dough with a cloth and leave in a warm place until it has doubled in size.

Knead again and divide into balls about the size of a medium apple.

Leave to prove for a further 10 minutes.

Add to a soup or stew for the last 20 minutes of cooking time, or boil in water.

Test the dumplings by sticking with a fork — if it comes out clean they are cooked.

# SHEEP'S HEAD BROTH

Serves 8-10

1 sheep's head
2-4 trotters
4 pints (2.25 litres/10 cups) water
Salt and pepper
A sprig each of parsley and thyme, chopped
2 onions
2 carrots
1 turnip
1 parsnip

Wash the head and trotters thoroughly and put them into a large saucepan.

Add some salt and pepper and the herbs.

Bring to the boil and simmer on a low heat for about 3 hours, or until the meat falls away from the bone.

Remove the head and trotters from the liquid.

Cut all the meat off the bone and chop it finely.

Chop all the vegetables into small pieces.

Return the meat and vegetables to the saucepan and simmer for a further hour.

Check the seasoning and serve hot.

# WESTERFIELD WHITE SOUP

Serves 4

This soup was particularly recommended for invalids.

1 lb (450 g) knuckle of veal
1 onion
1 level teaspoon salt
4 peppercorns
1 blade of mace
2 pints (1.15 litres/5 cups) water
¼ pint (150 ml/⅔ cup) cream
3 teaspoons arrowroot
A little milk
1 oz (25 g) cooked vermicelli
½ oz (15 g) blanched, slivered almonds

Put the knuckle of veal, sliced onion, salt, peppercorns and mace into a large saucepan and cover with the water.

Bring to the boil and simmer gently until the liquid has reduced by one-third — this will take 3-4 hours.

Strain the liquid and allow it to cool.

When it is cold, skim the fat from the surface.

Put the soup into a clean saucepan and bring to the boil.

Add the cream and the arrowroot mixed with a little milk.

Just before serving add the cooked vermicelli and almonds.

# IPSWICH PARTRIDGE SOUP

Serves 8

2 partridges
1 carrot, sliced
4 onions
12 cloves
4 oz (100 g) ham, finely chopped
3 pints (1.75 litres/7½ cups) stock
2 oz (50 g) softened butter
2 oz (50 g) flour
¼ pint (150 ml/⅔ cup) cream
Cayenne pepper

Roast the partridges in a moderately hot oven for 30-40 minutes, or until they are just cooked.

Crush the meat and bones and put into a large saucepan.

Add the sliced carrot, the onions stuck with cloves, and the ham.

Pour over the stock.

Bring to the boil, cover, and simmer slowly for 4 hours.

Strain the soup into a clean saucepan.

Mix the butter and flour together.

Add a little of the hot liquid to make a thin paste.

Stir this into the rest of the soup.

Bring to the boil and simmer for 10 minutes.

Stir in the cream, but do not re-boil.

Sprinkle with cayenne pepper before serving.

Oven: 375°F/190°C  Gas Mark 5

# FISH

From the fish huts on the beaches at Southwold, Dunwich and Aldeburgh the local catch can be bought at its freshest. Whiting is best in October and November, then cod through the winter until February. Plaice, sole and skate are at their peak during the spring and summer months.

Sprats are in season between October and March. You can buy them fresh and cook them yourself, or eat smoked ones with brown bread and butter and a slice of lemon in the local pub.

**To Cook Fresh Sprats**

Clean the fish thoroughly.

Sprinkle them with plenty of salt.

Heat a saucepan until it is really hot and toss in the salted sprats.

Fry them quickly for a couple of minutes on each side — the salt draws out the fat from the fish and this is what they cook in.

To eat the fish hold the head and tail between your fingers and nibble the flesh off the bone.

A sprinkling of lemon juice improves the flavour.

# WHITING

This is a traditional method of preparing the fish. Choose medium-sized, plump whiting, as the smaller ones are too bony.

Clean and wash the fish thoroughly.

Cover with plenty of salt and leave for 2 hours.

Hang the fish up to dry in the sun for 2 days.

To cook, boil them for 5-10 minutes in a pan of water.

Serve hot.

# BAKED STUFFED PLAICE

Serves 2

1 large plaice
3 tablespoons fresh white breadcrumbs
1 tablespoon finely chopped suet
1 tablespoon finely chopped parsley
½ teaspoon mixed dried herbs
A pinch of nutmeg
Salt and pepper
1 beaten egg
A little milk
1 tablespoon brown breadcrumbs
½ oz (15 g) butter

Wash the fish thoroughly.

Mix together the breadcrumbs, suet, parsley, herbs and nutmeg.

Season with salt and pepper.

Add half the egg and enough milk to moisten the breadcrumb mixture.

Make an incision down the centre of the fish, raise the flesh on each side and fill with the breadcrumb stuffing.

Brush the remaining beaten egg over the top of the fish and sprinkle in the brown breadcrumbs.

Put into a fireproof dish and dot the top with small pieces of butter.

Bake in a moderate oven for 25-30 minutes.

Oven: 350°F/180°C Gas Mark 4

# SMELTS

These small salt water fish used to be a great delicacy, but are now rather difficult to obtain. A fishmonger would probably be able to get them for you on order. Smelts should have a fresh smell, rather like cucumber, and a fine silvery colour. The flesh should be firm.

**Smelts**
**Seasoned flour**
**1 beaten egg**
**Breadcrumbs**
**Oil for deep-frying**

Wash the smelts, drain them well and pat dry with a piece of kitchen roll.

Toss in the seasoned flour.

Dip each smelt into the beaten egg and then coat with the breadcrumbs.

Deep-fry for a few minutes until golden brown.

# ALDEBURGH SPRATS

Serves 4

The first sprats of the season used to be sent to London for the Lord Mayor's Banquet.

**1 lb (450 g) sprats**
**1 oz (25 g) fine oatmeal**
**Salt**

Wash the sprats well and draw them.

Dust with the oatmeal.

Sprinkle a frying pan with salt and heat it — no fat will be needed as the salt draws the fat from the sprats.

Fry the sprats until they are golden brown.

# LOWESTOFT HERRINGS WITH MUSTARD SAUCE

Serves 4

**4 herrings**

**For the mustard sauce:**
**1 oz (25 g) flour**
**A pinch of salt**
**½ pint (300 ml/1¼ cups) milk**
**1 oz (25 g) sugar**
**½ oz (15 g) butter**
**1 teaspoon mustard powder**
**Vinegar**

Clean and gut the herrings.

Bring a large pan of salted water to the boil and put in the herrings.

Boil for 10 minutes.

**To make the sauce:**

Mix the flour and salt with a little milk to make a paste, then gradually add the rest of the milk, stirring to prevent lumps.

Put a drop of water in a saucepan and bring to the boil, then add the milk mixture and stir over a low heat until it thickens.

Stir in the sugar and butter, and then the mustard powder mixed with vinegar.

Drain the herrings and serve hot with the mustard sauce.

# FILLETS OF SOLE
# WITH MUSHROOMS

Serves 4

**8 fillets of sole**
**Salt and pepper**
**2 teaspoons lemon juice**
**2 tablespoons white wine**
**2 tablespoons water**
**6 oz (175 g) button mushrooms**
**1 oz (25 g) butter**
**1 oz (25 g) flour**
**4 tablespoons milk**
**Chopped parsley for decoration**

Wash the fillets and pat them dry.

Season with salt and pepper, and sprinkle one teaspoon of lemon juice over them all.

Fold each fillet into three and place in an ovenproof dish.

Add the wine and water.

Cover and cook in a moderately hot oven for 20 minutes.

Put the mushrooms in a separate dish with a little water, a pinch of salt and one teaspoon of lemon juice.

Cover and cook at the same time as the fish.

Melt the butter in a saucepan and stir in the flour, cooking for 1 minute without browning.

Gradually add the milk, the liquid from the mushrooms, and enough of the fish liquor to make a smooth sauce.

Arrange the fillets around the edge of a serving dish and coat with the sauce.

Pile the mushrooms in the centre.

Sprinkle with chopped parsley.

Oven: 375°F/190°C  Gas Mark 5

# KIPPER PASTE

**1 large kipper**
**4 oz (100 g) unsalted butter**
**2 hard-boiled eggs**
**Clarified butter**

Fill a tall jug with boiling water and stand the kipper in it, head down, for 10 minutes.

Remove the flesh from the bones.

Soften the butter.

Pound the butter and kipper flesh together.

Mash the hard-boiled eggs and pound into the kipper mixture — this can be done in a liquidizer.

Pack the paste into individual dishes.

Pour clarified butter over the top to seal.

# KIPPER SAVOURY

Serves 4

**2 large kippers**
**2 oz (50 g) butter**
**1 tablespoon chopped chives**
**A clove of garlic, crushed**

**For the pastry:**
**8 oz (225 g) plain flour**
**3 oz (75 g) lard**
**3 oz (75 g) peeled and grated raw potato**
**A little water**

Simmer the kippers in boiling water until the flesh comes away from the bones easily.

Soften the butter in a basin and add the flaked kipper, chives and garlic.

**To make the pastry:**

Sift the flour into a mixing basin and rub in the lard.

Add the potato and enough water to make a firm dough.

Roll out half the dough to line a greased 8 inch (20 cm) pie plate.

Spoon in the kipper filling.

Roll out the other half of the dough to make a lid.

Dampen the edges of the pastry, press them together to seal, then trim and flute with a knife.

Make a criss-cross pattern on top of the pie with a sharp knife, cutting through the pastry.

Brush with melted butter.

Bake in a moderately hot oven for 30-40 minutes until golden brown.

Oven: 400°F/200°C  Gas Mark 6

# FRIED SKATE WITH
# TOMATO SAUCE

Serves 4

1½ lbs (675 g) wing of skate
1 egg
**Breadcrumbs**
Fat or oil for frying

**For the tomato sauce:**
1 onion
1 small carrot
1 rasher of streaky bacon
½ oz (15 g) butter
4 medium-sized tomatoes
½ oz (15 g) flour
½ pint (300 ml/ 1¼ cups) light stock
**Salt and pepper**
1 teaspoon lemon juice
1 level teaspoon sugar
**A pinch of grated nutmeg**

Cut the skate into neat pieces and simmer in salted water for 5 minutes.

Drain and dry.

Coat each piece with beaten egg and then breadcrumbs, pressing the coating on firmly.

Fry in hot fat or oil until golden brown, turning once during cooking.

Pat dry with absorbent kitchen paper, and keep warm.

**To make the tomato sauce:**

Slice the onion and carrot.

Chop the bacon into small pieces.

Melt the butter in a saucepan and fry the onion, carrot and bacon gently for 10 minutes.

Slice the tomatoes and add them to the saucepan.

Cook for a further 5 minutes.

Sprinkle on the flour add the stock and stir until the sauce boils.

Simmer for 45 minutes.

Rub the sauce through a sieve, or use a liquidizer, and then re-heat.

Season with salt and pepper.

Add the lemon juice, sugar and nutmeg.

Pour over the skate, and serve.

# SUFFOLK TROUT

**4 river trout**
**4 bay leaves**
**2 oz (50 g) butter**
**Juice of 1 lemon**

Remove the heads of the fish and clean them thoroughly, inside and out.

Put a bay leaf inside each fish.

Melt the butter in a large frying pan with a lid.

Put in the trout.

Sprinkle with lemon juice.

Cover and cook on a low heat for about 20 minutes, turning once, until the flesh comes away from the bone.

# EEL PIE

**2 lbs (900 g) eel**
**2 oz (50 g) flour**
**Salt and pepper**
**2 oz (50 g) butter**
**1 onion**
**1 glass of white wine**
**1 teaspoon chopped fennel**
**1 teaspoon chopped parsley**
**Grated rind and juice of 1 lemon**
**¼ pint (150 ml/⅔ cup) cream**
**2 hard-boiled eggs**
**8 oz (225 g) puff pastry**

Cut the eel into 2 inch (5 cm) pieces.

Toss in the flour seasoned with salt and pepper.

Melt the butter in a frying pan and fry the eel until golden brown.

Lift out with a perforated spoon and put into a pie dish.

Fry the sliced onion in the remaining butter.

Sprinkle over any remaining flour, cool for a minute, then add the wine, herbs, lemon rind and juice.

Stir in the cream and season with salt and pepper.

Strain the sauce over the eel in the pie dish.

Slice the hard-boiled eggs and put on top of the eel.

Roll out the pastry to make a lid.

Use any scraps of pastry to decorate the top, and brush with milk or beaten egg to glaze.

Bake in a hot oven for 20 minutes, then reduce the temperature and bake for a further 40 minutes.

Oven: 425°°F/220°C  Gas Mark 7
Reduce to: 350°F/180°C  Gas Mark 4

# SHRIMP PIE

**1 quart (1.15 litres/ 5 cups) shrimps**
**3 anchovies**
**A pinch of mace**
**1 oz (25 g) butter**
**1 glass dry white wine**
**4 oz (100 g) shortcrust pastry**

Shell the shrimps.

Bone and mince the anchovies.

Mix together the shrimps, minced anchovies and a pinch of mace.

Put half the butter in small pieces in the bottom of a pie plate.

Put in the shrimp mixture with the rest of the butter on top (in small pieces).

Pour over the glass of wine.

Roll out the pastry until it is very thin, and cover the pie.

Bake in a moderately hot oven for 10-15 minutes, or until the piecrust is golden brown.

Oven: 400°F/200°C  Gas Mark 6

# POTTED SHRIMPS

Before the advent of the deep-freeze, 'potting' was an important method of preserving meat and fish. The spices and the seal of clarified butter were the chief preserving agents. Prawns, lobsters, crabs or crayfish may also be prepared in the following way.

1 lb (450 g) shelled shrimps (or other shellfish)
8 oz (225 g) butter
1 teaspoon mace
½ teaspoon powdered ginger
A pinch of salt
A pinch of cayenne pepper

Finely chop half the shrimps and leave the other half whole.

Melt 6 oz (175 g) of the butter and stir in the shrimps.

Add the mace, ginger, salt and cayenne pepper.

Stir over a low heat until all the butter is absorbed into the mixture.

Spoon the mixture into small jars or moulds.

While still hot, melt the rest of the butter and pour over the top.

Leave overnight to cool.

Turn out to serve, with hot toast.

# STEWED OYSTERS

2 dozen oysters
A pinch of mace
A few slivers of lemon peel
6 white peppercorns
¼ pint (150 ml/ ⅔ cup) cream
½ oz (15 g) softened butter
½ oz (15 g) flour
Sippets of toast

Open the shells and separate the liquor from the oysters.

Beard the oysters.

Strain the liquor into a saucepan and add the oysters, mace, lemon peel and peppercorns.

Simmer very gently for 5 minutes.

Remove the lemon peel and peppercorns and add the cream.

Cream the butter and flour together to form a ball and add this to the saucepan.

Simmer for a further 5 minutes.

Serve piping hot with sippets of toast.

**To make fried sippets:**

Cut stale bread into small cubes and fry in hot oil in a frying basket until golden brown.

# OYSTER HOT POT

Serves 4

1 lb (450 g) braising steak
2 oz (50 g) lard
2 lamb's kidneys
12 oysters
1 onion
1 oz (25 g) flour
1 pint (600 ml/ 2½ cups) water
1½ lbs (675 g) potatoes
Salt and pepper

Cut the steak into ½ inch (1 cm) pieces and brown them in the melted lard.

Transfer to a casserole.

Skin and slice the kidneys and add to the steak.

Add the oysters, reserving any liquor for the sauce.

Peel and slice the potatoes and cover the mixture in the casserole with them.

Slice the onion and fry in the remaining fat.

Sprinkle over the flour, cook for a couple of minutes, then add the water and the liquor from the oysters.

Bring to the boil, stirring all the time, so that the sauce thickens.

Pour the sauce over the casserole, and season to taste.

Cover and cook in a moderate oven for 1½ hours.

Remove the lid and continue cooking for another 30 minutes so that the potatoes brown.

Oven: 350°F/180°C  Gas Mark 4

# PILLAR OF RICE

Serves 4

This is an unusual way of using up left-over chicken or turkey — or any sort of game. The name comes from the shape into which the rice is moulded.

**8-12 oz (225 - 350 g) left-over chicken, turkey, or any game meat**
**½ pint (300 ml/ 1¼ cups) cold stock or gravy**
**Salt and pepper**
**12 oz (350 g) cooked rice**
**2 oz (50 g) fresh white breadcrumbs**
**1 oz (25 g) butter**

Put the cold cooked meat into an ovenproof pie dish.

Pour over the stock.

Season well with salt and pepper.

Pile on the cooked rice, shaping it into a dome or 'pillar'.

Sprinkle over the breadcrumbs.

Dot all over with small pieces of butter.

Bake in a hot oven for about 45 minutes, until nicely browned.

Oven: 425°F/220°C  Gas Mark 7

# STUFFED GUINEA FOWL

Serves 4

The celery and watercress 'stuffing' in this recipe is used for flavouring only — it is not eaten as part of the dish.

**2 small guinea fowl**
**1 stick of celery**
**3 sprigs of watercress**
**1 clove of garlic**
**Salt and pepper**
**3 oz (75 g) butter**
**1 lemon**
**A glass of dry white wine**
**½ pint (300 ml/1¼ cups) stock**
**2 egg yolks**

Chop the celery and watercress, crush the garlic, and bind them all together with 1 oz (25 g) of the butter.

Season with salt and pepper and put into the birds.

Grate the lemon rind, mix with salt and pepper, and rub over the skin of the guinea fowl.

Melt 2 oz (50 g) of the butter in a large pan and brown the birds in it.

Pour in the wine and stock and bring to the boil.

Cover and simmer for about 45 minutes.

Lift out the guinea fowl, drain, and remove the stuffing.

Joint each bird into halves, put on a serving dish and keep warm.

Beat the juice from the lemon and the egg yolks together.

Add a little of the hot stock, then pour into the pan.

Heat through gently without boiling until the sauce has thickened.

Pour the sauce over the guinea fowl and garnish with lemon slices.

# ROAST STUFFED GOOSE

Michaelmas Day used to be observed in Suffolk on October 11th, known as Old Michaelmas. Everyone who could afford it had a roast goose for dinner. In fact if you did not baste a goose on this day 'you would want for money all the year'.

**1 goose, weighing about 8-10 lbs (3.5-4.5 kg)**

**For the stuffing:**
**2 onions**
**2 cups of fresh white breadcrumbs**
**Salt and pepper**
**1 goose liver**
**3 egg yolks**

Calculate the roasting time for the goose — 15 minutes per lb (450 g) plus 15 minutes.

Pre-heat the oven.

Wash the goose thoroughly, inside and out, and pat dry.

Put the giblets into a saucepan and cover with water.

Bring to the boil and simmer for a couple of minutes, then remove the liver to add to the stuffing — the rest of the giblets will be used for the gravy.

Chop the onions and the goose liver very finely and mix with the breadcrumbs.

Season well with salt and pepper.

Stir in the egg yolks to bind the stuffing together, and put it into the goose.

Truss the goose and prick the skin of the breast.

Put into the pre-heated oven and roast for the appropriate time — you may wish to pour off the accumulated fat from time to time.

When it is almost cooked, dredge the breast with flour and baste with some of the hot fat.

Serve with apple sauce, and gravy made from the giblets.

Oven: 400°F/200°C  Gas Mark 6

# SUFFOLK JUGGED HARE

Serves 6-8

Hare is in season from September to the end of February. This dish gets its name from the deep, lidded stoneware jug in which it was traditionally cooked.

**1 hare**
**A little flour**
**2 onions**
**6 cloves**
**A sprig each of parsley and thyme**
**6 each whole allspice and peppercorns**
**A strip of lemon peel**
**A glass of port wine**

Prepare the hare and cut into small joints.

Dust the joints with flour and put into a saucepan.

Add the onions stuck with cloves, chopped herbs, the allspice, peppercorns and lemon peel.

Cover with water, bring to the boil and simmer for about 2 hours until the meat is tender.

Lift out the pieces of meat and place on a serving dish.

Thicken the stock with a tablespoonful of flour mixed with a little water.

Add the glass of port.

Boil for another five minutes, then strain through a sieve and pour over the hare.

Serve with redcurrant jelly.

# RABBIT PIE

**1 rabbit**
**2 onions**
**Seasoned flour**
**12 oz (350 g) belly pork**
**Chopped parsley and sage**
**12 oz (350 g) puff pastry**
**Beaten egg or a little milk to glaze**

Bone the rabbit, and cut the meat into portions.

Soak the meat in cold water for an hour to whiten it.

Meanwhile, put into a saucepan the bones and one of the onions, roughly chopped.

Cover with water, season with salt and pepper, and bring to the boil.

Simmer for at least an hour.

Lift the rabbit portions out with a perforated spoon and wipe dry.

Dredge with seasoned flour and put into a large pie dish.

Cut the pork into pieces and add them to the dish.

Sprinkle with chopped parsley, sage and the remaining onion.

Add enough stock from boiling the bones to come three-quarters of the way up the dish.

Roll out the pastry to make a lid and make a hole in the top.

Brush with beaten egg or milk to glaze.

Bake in a moderately hot oven for ½ an hour, then reduce the heat and continue cooking for a further hour.

The pie is eaten cold.

Oven: 375°F/190°C  Gas Mark 5
Reduce to: 325°F/160°C  Gas Mark 3

# PORK

Every country family used to keep a pig, and until after the Second World War pork was the only 'carcase' meat that most of them ate. The autumn pig-killing was an important event. Nothing was ever wasted, the most perishable parts being used up first. The offal — a mixture of the liver, kidney, belly, heart and brain — was used in a dish called pigs' fry. The head was turned into brawn. Joints were salted, hams cured for the winter months ahead, and odd pieces were made into sausages and pies. Even the chitterlings — intestines — were boiled and eaten either hot or cold, or they were cut up and mixed with apples and currants as a filling for a pastry turnover.

## SUFFOLK SAUSAGES
Serves 4

1 lb (450 g) minced pork
1 oz (25 g) fresh white breadcrumbs
A pinch of mace, powdered cloves and nutmeg
Salt and pepper
Sausage skins

Mix all the ingredients well, adding a little water if the mixture is too dry.

Season with salt and pepper.

Put the mixture into the skins.

Boil the sausages for about 10 minutes before frying them.

# SOUTHWOLD DUMPLING

Serves 6-8

2 lbs (900 g) leg of pork
1 lb (450 g) onions
Salt and pepper
12 oz (350 g) self-raising flour
6 oz (175 g) shredded suet
A pinch of salt
About 8 fl oz (250 ml/1 cup) cold water

Grease a large pudding basin.

Mix together the flour, suet and salt, and add enough cold water to make a pliable dough.

Roll out the dough and line the basin, reserving a piece to make the lid.

Cut the pork into small pieces.

Peel and slice the onions.

Arrange the pork and slice the onion inside the suet crust in alternate layers.

When full, pour over ¼ pint (150 ml/ ⅔ cup) water.

Put on the suet crust lid, pressing the edges firmly together.

Cover the basin with greaseproof paper and aluminium foil, securely tied.

Steam for 4-5 hours.

# BRAWN

1 pig's head
Tongue, heart and liver
10 peppercorns
6 cloves
1 cup of vinegar
1 onion, chopped
1 teaspoon dried sage
Pepper

Clean the pig's head thoroughly and soak it in brine for a few days.

Wash well in clean cold water.

Put the head into a large pan and cover with water.

Bring to the boil and simmer for 1½-2 hours, until the meat drops from the bone.

Boil the tongue, heart and liver in a separate pan until soft.

Strain off the stock, and add to the cooking liquid from the head.

Add the peppercorns and cloves, bring to the boil and boil rapidly until the liquid is reduced to 1 pint (600 ml/ 2½ cups).

Strain, and add the cupful of vinegar.

Chop up all the meat and add the chopped onion and the sage.

Season with pepper.

Pack the meat into dishes and pour the stock over.

Weight down well and leave a few days before eating.

# PIG'S FRY

Serves 4

1 lb (450 g) pig's fry
1 oz (25 g) pork fat
2 sliced onions
1 tablespoon chopped sage
Salt and pepper
1 oz (25 g) cornflour

Cut the fry into small pieces and place in an ovenproof dish.

Add the pork fat, sliced onions and chopped sage.

Season with salt and pepper.

Bake in a moderate oven for about 1½ hours.

Strain off the cooking liquid into a saucepan.

Mix the cornflour with a little water and add to the cooking liquid.

Bring to the boil, stirring, until the gravy has thickened.

Pour over the pig's fry and serve hot.

Oven: 350°F/180°C  Gas Mark 4

# SUFFOLK SWEET CURED HAM

Most Suffolk households kept their own pig and had a large earthenware ham pot, glazed on the inside, in which the pork was cured, first in salt and then in a sweet pickle of treacle or honey. After curing, the hams were sent to be dried in the 'Smokey House'. This was usually owned by the local cooper, who used up his sawdust. The sawdust was damped to make it smoke a lot, and the hams were hung there for about three weeks.

**A freshly-cut ham**
**Salt**
**Saltpetre**
**1 gallon (4.5 litres) water**
**2 lbs (1 kg) black treacle**
**1 lb (450 g) cooking salt**
**1 lb (450 g) brown sugar**
**1 oz (25 g) black pepper**

Use 1 oz (25 g) saltpetre to each 1 lb (450 g) salt, and rub the mixture well into the freshly-cut ham.

Leave for one week.

Put all the other ingredients into a large pan, bring to the boil and simmer for about 20 minutes.

Leave until cold, then pour over the dry-salted ham.

Cover and leave for 4-6 weeks, depending on the size of the ham.

Hang in the chimney breast for at least three weeks.

The ham will then be ready to eat, but will keep for at least a year.

# POTTED HAM

This potted ham will keep for about six weeks in the refrigerator, or it can be deep frozen and kept for several months.

**8 oz (225 g) onions**
**1 oz (25 g) butter**
**1 lb (450 g) cooked ham**
**1 teaspoon paprika**
**½ teaspoon cayenne pepper**
**A glass of cider or red wine**
**Clarified butter**

Thinly slice the onions.

Melt the butter in a pan and fry the onion slowly until soft.

Mince the ham and the onion together.

Season with curry powder, paprika, cayenne pepper and add salt if necessary.

Put the ham mixture into a saucepan, stir in the cider or wine and simmer over a low heat for 30 minutes.

Allow to cool.

Use the blender to reduce the mixture to a smooth paste.

Spoon the paste into small jars or moulds and seal with clarified butter.

**To clarify the butter:**

Heat slightly salted butter gently in saucepan, stirring all the time until the liquid foams.

Cook without browning, until the foaming stops.

Allow to stand for a few minutes, but not to solidify.

Strain through muslin before serving.

# GAMMON AND TURNIP PIE

Serves 4

**3 lbs (1½ kg) young turnips**
**4 gammon steaks**
**2 oz (50 g) butter**
**½ pint (300 ml/ 1¼ cups) cream**
**4 oz (100 g) fresh white breadcrumbs**
**4 oz (100 g) grated Cheddar cheese**
**Salt and pepper**

Scrub the turnips thoroughly and put into a pan of water.

Add a pinch of salt and bring to the boil.

Cover, and simmer until the turnips are tender.

Drain and leave to cool.

When cool, peel the turnips and cut them into ½ inch (1 cm) cubes.

Melt the butter in a frying pan and fry the gammon steaks on both sides.

Cut the gammon into cubes.

Pour the juices from the frying pan into an ovenproof dish, brushing all round the sides.

Put the turnip and gammon into the dish in layers, seasoning each layer with salt and pepper.

Pour over the cream.

Mix the breadcrumbs and cheese together and spread over the top.

Dot with a few knobs of butter.

Place under a hot grill until the top is brown and bubbling.

# LAYER PUDDING

Serves 6-8

An unusual and filling way of using up cooked, left-over meat from the joint.

**12 oz (350 g) self-raising flour**
**4 oz (100 g) suet**
**A pinch of salt**
**Water**
**1 lb (450 g) cooked lamb or pork**
**1 onion**
**Salt and pepper**
**2 tablespoons stock or gravy**

Mix together the flour, suet and salt, and add enough water to make a firm pastry.

Use half the suet pastry to line a greased pudding basin.

Chop the cooked meat and the onions finely and mix them together.

Season well with salt and pepper.

Add a little stock or gravy to moisten.

Put a layer of the meat mixture into the basin.

From the remaining pastry, roll out thin circles.

Put one on top of the meat.

Continue alternately with the meat mixture and the circles of suet pastry until both are used up, finishing with a pastry layer.

Cover the pudding with grease proof paper, tied securely.

Serve hot with gravy.

# LEG OF LAMB WITH DUMPLINGS

Serves 6-8

A 2 lb (900 g) leg of lamb
1 lb (450 g) carrots
8 oz (225 g) onions
2 oz (50 g) butter or lard
1 pint (600 ml/ 2½ cups) stock
A sprig of parsley
Salt and pepper

For the dumplings:
4 oz (100 g) self-raising flour
2 oz (50 g) shredded suet
A pinch of salt
Water
1 oz (25 g) cornflour

Wipe and trim the lamb.

Chop the carrots and slice the onions.

Melt the butter in a large saucepan and fry the carrots and onions for 10 minutes.

Place the leg of lamb on top of the vegetables.

Pour over the stock.

Chop the parsley and add to the saucepan.

Season with salt and pepper.

Bring to the boil, cover with a lid and simmer on a low heat for 1-1½ hours, until the meat is tender.

**To make the dumplings:**

Mix together the flour, shredded suet and salt.

Add enough water to bind the ingredients together.

Shape the dough into 8 small balls.

Add the dumplings to the saucepan 15 minutes before the end of cooking time.

When everything is cooked, lift the meat, vegetables and dumplings onto a serving dish.

Blend the cornflour with a little water and stir into the gravy to thicken it.

Serve the gravy with the meat, vegetables and dumplings.

# OXTAIL BRAWN

**1 oxtail**
**A little flour**
**1 oz (25 g) butter**
**1 onion stuck with 3 cloves**
**2 tablespoons vinegar**
**A sprig of parsley and thyme**
**Salt and pepper**
**1 hard-boiled egg**

Cut the oxtail into pieces, dust with flour and brown in the melted butter.

Put into a large saucepan with the onion, vinegar and herbs and cover with water.

Season with salt and pepper.

Bring to the boil, cover, and simmer for 3-4 hours until the meats comes away from the bone.

Separate the meat from the bones and put the bones back into the stock.

Boil rapidly until it has reduced to ½ pint (300 ml/ 1¼ cups).

Chop the meat and put into a buttered mould.

Decorate the top with the sliced hard-boiled egg.

Pour over the reduced stock.

Leave until cold.

Turn out onto a serving dish.

# DRESSMAKER TRIPE

Serves 4

The name of this dish reflects the fact the the tripe is sewn up at the edges to contain the stuffing.

**A piece of prepared tripe, about 1-1½ lbs (450-675 g)**
**1 large onion**
**4 oz (100 g) fresh white breadcrumbs**
**A sprig of parsley and thyme, chopped.**
**Salt and pepper**
**4 slices of streaky bacon**

Boil the onion until it is soft.

Mix the boiled onion, breadcrumbs and chopped herbs together to make the stuffing.

Season with salt and pepper.

Spread the stuffing over half the piece of tripe and fold the other half on top of it.

Sew the edges of the tripe together.

Put the tripe in a greased baking tin and lay the slices of bacon on top.

Bake in a moderate oven for 1 hour.

Serve with a good brown gravy.

Oven: 350°F/180°C  Gas Mark 4

# SAMPHIRE

Samphire grows wild on the coastal marshes and mud flats around Walberswick and Southwold. It is an odd-looking, succulent plant rather like asparagus, and is also known locally as glasswort, saltwort, pickle plant or crabgrass. You can eat samphire raw as a salad vegetable when it is young and tender, or boil it in unsalted water for five minutes and add a knob of butter.

Traditionally, samphire was eaten hot with mutton or lamb — the sheep having grazed on samphire while it was growing on the marshes. It was the custom to serve meat with the food on which the animal had fed.

You can still buy samphire in selected shops in East Anglia, but the best way is to gather it yourself when the tide is out. July and August are the best months, when the plants are about to flower.

# SUFFOLK CARROT PIE

Serves 4

*Served hot, this tasty dish makes an excellent accompaniment to cold meats.*

**6 carrots**
**6 potatoes**
**2 eggs, separated**
**Salt and pepper**
**2 tablespoons plain flour**

Grease an ovenproof dish.

Grate the carrots and potatoes.

Beat the egg yolks and season with salt and pepper.

Gradually stir in the flour to make a smooth paste.

Blend the grated carrots and potatoes into the egg mixture.

Beat the egg whites until they form stiff peaks and fold into the mixture.

Turn the mixture into the greased dish and bake in a moderate oven for about 40 minutes, until golden brown.

Oven: 350°F/180°C  Gas Mark 4

# STEWED RED CABBAGE

This is an excellent vegetable to serve with sausages.

**1 small red cabbage**
**1 slice of ham, diced**
**½ oz (15 g) butter**
**¾ pint (450 ml/ 2 cups) stock**
**¼ pint (150 ml/ ⅔ cup) vinegar**
**Salt and pepper**
**1 tablespoon caster sugar**

Cut the cabbage into quarters and wash thoroughly.

Slice very thinly.

Put into a large saucepan with the diced ham, butter, ½ pint (300 ml/ 1¼ cups) of stock and the vinegar.

Bring to the boil, cover, and simmer gently for about 1 hour, or until the cabbage is tender.

Add the rest of the stock, and the sugar.

Season with salt and pepper.

Mix well and stir in over the heat until nearly all the liquid has evaporated.

Serve hot.

# STEWED ENDIVE

**6 heads of endive**
**1 oz (25 g) butter**
**1 oz (25 g) flour**
**¾ pint (450 ml/ 2 cups) stock**
**1 tablespoon lemon juice**
**Salt and pepper**

Cut the stumps off the endive and discard any tough outer leaves.

Wash thoroughly.

Boil in salted water for 10 minutes to blanch the endive and remove the bitter flavour.

Drain well and chop finely.

Melt the butter in a saucepan and stir in the flour.

Cook gently for a couple of minutes without browning.

Add the stock, stirring until the sauce is boiling.

Add the lemon juice and season with salt and pepper.

Add the chopped endive and simmer until heated through.

Serve hot.

# CHITTERLING TURNOVER

Serves 6-8

In the autumn when the pig was killed, hams were prepared for the winter ahead, but the perishable parts were used up immediately. Chitterlings are the small intestines of the pig, and were boiled and eaten either hot or cold, or cut up and mixed with apples and currants as a filling for a pastry turnover.

**12 oz (350 g) shortcrust or puff pastry**
**Pig's chitterlings**
**3 cooking apples**
**3 oz (75 g) currants**
**Sugar**
**1 level teaspoon mixed spice**

Roll out the pastry to a rectangular shape about 10 inches x 6 inches (25 cm x 15 cm).

Clean the chitterlings thoroughly, put them in a saucepan covered with water and simmer until tender.

Chop the chitterlings finely.

Peel, core and chop the apples.

Mix the apples, currants, spice and sugar according to taste.

Spoon this mixture onto one half of the pastry, turn the other half over it and press down the edges.

Place on a baking sheet and bake in a moderately hot oven for 40-45 minutes, until the pastry is golden brown.

Oven: 375°F/190°C Gas Mark 5

# ELDERFLOWER FRITTERS

Serves 4

The countryside around East Bergholt in Suffolk is known as Constable country. Many of his works include elderberry bushes — he had a particular passion for painting the creamy panicles of the elderflower.

**2 or 3 elderflower heads per person**
**4 oz (100 g) plain flour**
**A pinch of salt**
**1 egg**
**¼ pint (150 ml/⅔ cup) milk**
**Butter**
**Caster sugar**

Sift the flour and salt into a mixing basin.

Make a well in the centre and break in the egg.

Work in the flour from the sides, gradually adding the milk a little at a time until you have a smooth mixture free from lumps.

Beat thoroughly.

Heat a frying pan until it is really hot and add a knob of butter.

Dip the elderflower heads in the batter, holding them by the stalks.

Fry until crisp.

Serve immediately, sprinkled with caster sugar.

49

# TREACLE CUSTARD TART

Serves 6

**6 oz (175 g) golden syrup**
**2 eggs**
**6 oz (175 g) shortcrust pastry**

**For the shortcrust pastry:**
**4 oz (100 g) plain flour**
**2 oz (50 g) butter**
**A pinch of salt**
**1 dessertspoon sugar**
**Water to mix**

**To make rich shortcrust pastry:**

Sift the flour.

Break the butter into pieces and work lightly into the flour.

Mix with the salt and sugar.

Add sufficient water to make a firm dough.

Roll out on a floured surface.

**To make the filling:**

Warm the syrup and mix with the beaten eggs.

Leave to cool.

Roll out the pastry to line a greased 8 inch (20 cm) pie plate.

Spoon the filling into the pastry base.

Bake in a moderately hot oven for 30-40 minutes until golden brown.

Serve cold.

Oven: 375°F/190°C  Gas Mark 5

# GREENGAGE TART

Serves 4-6

Sir William Gage, who lived at Hengrave Hall in Suffolk, gave his name to the green plum.

**1 lb (450 g) greengages**
**Approx 2 oz (50 g) sugar**
**8 oz (225 g) shortcrust pastry**

Roll out half the pastry and line a greased 8 inch (20 cm) pie plate.

Trim the edges.

Roll out the remaining pastry to fit the top of the plate.

Halve and stone the greengages and pack into the pie plate.

Sprinkle with sugar.

Dampen the edges of the pastry base.

Place on the lid and press the edges firmly together.

Trim and flute the edges.

Make a couple of slits in the top to allow the steam to escape.

Bake in a hot oven for 15 minutes until the pastry is lightly coloured, then reduce the temperature and continue baking for another 30 minutes.

Sprinkle with caster sugar and serve hot or cold, with custard or cream.

Oven: 425°F/220°C  Gas Mark 7
Reduce to: 325°F/160°C  Gas Mark 3

# FELIXSTOWE TART

1½ lbs (675 g) cooking apples
4 oz (100 g) plain flour
4 oz (100 g) cornflour
1 teaspoon baking powder
3 oz (75 g) butter
3 oz (75 g) granulated sugar
2 eggs, separated
3 oz (75 g) caster sugar

Peel, core and slice the apples and put into a saucepan with a little water and sugar to taste.

Cook gently until soft.

Leave to cool.

Meanwhile sift the flours and baking powder into a mixing basin.

Cut the butter into small pieces and rub into the flour.

Add the granulated sugar.

Bind together with the egg yolks.

Roll out the pastry on a floured surface.

Line a greased 10 inch (25 cm) pie plate.

Prick the base, line with greaseproof paper and fill with baking beans.

Bake "blind" in a moderate oven for 20 minutes.

Remove the paper and beans and leave to cool.

Spoon in the cooked apple.

Whip the egg whites until they stand in peaks and fold in the caster sugar.

Pile on top of the apple.

Bake in a cool oven until the meringue is set and lightly browned.

Serve hot or cold with cream.

Oven: 350°F/180°C Gas Mark 4
Reduce to: 275°F/140°C Gas Mark 1

# THAPE PIE

Thape is an old Suffolk word for gooseberry. Whit Sunday was celebrated with gooseberry or thape pie and with baked custards.

**1½ lbs (675 g) gooseberries**
**4 oz (100 g) sugar**
**2 tablespoons water**
**6 oz (175 g) shortcrust pastry**

Top and tail the gooseberries and wash them well.

Put half of them into a 1½ pint (900 ml) pie dish.

Add the sugar and water.

Pile on the rest of the gooseberries.

Roll out the pastry into a circle about ½ inch (1 cm) larger than the pie dish.

Trim off the surplus to line the edge of the dish.

Dampen the edge before covering with the pastry lid.

Press the edges of the pastry firmly together to seal.

Bake in a hot oven for 15 minutes until the pastry is set, then reduce the heat and continue cooking for another 30 minutes until the fruit is tender.

Dredge with caster sugar before serving.

Oven: 425°F/220°C  Gas Mark 7
Reduce to: 350°F/180°C  Gas Mark 4

# IPSWICH ALMOND PUDDING      Serves 6-8

The original 18th century recipe is for a rich custard filling over a puff pastry base.

¾ pint (450 ml/2 cups) milk
¼ pint (150 ml/⅔ cup) double cream
2 oz (50 g) fresh white breadcrumbs
3 oz (75 g) caster sugar
6 oz (175 g) ground almonds
1 teaspoon rosewater
3 eggs
1 oz (25 g) butter

Warm the milk and cream.

Pour over the breadcrumbs.

Stir in the sugar, ground almonds and rosewater.

Beat the eggs and blend thoroughly with the mixture.

Pour into a buttered ovenproof dish.

Dot with butter.

Stand the dish in a roasting tin half full of water.

Bake in a moderate oven for 30 minutes, until set.

Oven: 350°F/180°C  Gas Mark 4

# MOTHERING SUNDAY PUDDING     Serves 8

This recipe comes from Hadleigh in Suffolk. It used to be served on Mothering Sunday, when daughters who were away from home in service came home to see their mothers. The pudding used to be boiled in a scalded pudding cloth, but these days steaming it in a basin covered with greaseproof paper or aluminium foil will do just as well. If you use a pressure cooker the time will be considerably reduced.

**8 oz (225 g) flour**
**8 oz (225 g) shredded suet**
**8 oz (225 g) raisins**
**2 oz (50 g) sugar**
**2 eggs**

Grease and flour a 2 pint (1.15 litre/5 cups) pudding basin.

Mix together the flour, suet, raisins and sugar.

Beat the eggs and stir into the dry ingredients to bind them together.

Put the mixture into the pudding basin, making sure there is space for it to expand.

Cover with a double thickness of greaseproof paper, tied securely, or with aluminium foil.

Place the basin in a saucepan of water and steam for about 3-4 hours, until the pudding is well risen.

# NEWMARKET PUDDING

3 oz (75 g) sugar
2 eggs
½ pint (300 ml/1¼ cups) milk
5 individual sponge cakes
2 oz (50 g) raisins
2 oz (50 g) currants
1 oz (25 g) cut mixed peel
3 tablespoons redcurrant jelly

Beat the sugar and eggs together.

Stir in the milk.

Slice the sponge cakes in half.

Grease a pudding basin and put a layer of sponge cake in the bottom, followed by a layer of the mixed dried fruit and peel.

Continue with these layers until all the ingredients are used up.

Pour over the custard mixture.

Cover the basin with greaseproof paper and a pudding cloth or aluminium foil.

Place in a saucepan of boiling water and steam for 1-1¼ hours, or until the custard is set.

Turn the pudding out before serving.

Warm the redcurrant jelly and spoon it over the top.

# STRAWBERRIES IN WINE

Before the days of the deep-freeze, strawberries and other soft fruit used to be preserved in wine, providing a delicious dessert long after the summer was over.

**Strawberries**
**Caster sugar**
**Madeira, sherry, or homemade orange wine**

Hull the fruit and arrange in layers in a Kilner fruit-bottling jar, or any wide-necked bottle.

Sprinkle a little sugar over each layer.

Fill up the jar with wine.

Put on the lid, making sure it is securely fastened.

The fruit can be left for several months before eating.

# STRAWBERRY AND RASPBERRY FOOL

Serves 8

1 pint (600 ml/ 2½ cups) ripe strawberries
1 pint (600 ml/2½ cups) raspberries
8 oz (225 g) caster sugar
1 tablespoon orange-flower water (A little fresh orange
  juice would do)
1½ pints (900 ml/ 3¾ cups) cream
Strawberries for decoration

Bruise the strawberries and raspberries and pass them through a sieve.

Mix in the sugar and orange-flower water.

Boil the cream and stir it until it is cold.

Beat the fruit pulp and the cold cream together until they are well mixed.

Spoon the fool into individual glasses and decorate with whole strawberries.

# GOOSEBERRY CREAM

The following recipe comes from a cookery book that belonged to Oliver Cromwell's wife, in the 17th century.

'First boyl, or you may preserve your Gooseberries, then having a clear Cream boyled up and seasoned with old Cinamon, Nutmeg, Mace, Sugar, Rosewater and Eggs, dish it up, and when it is cold take up the Gooseberries with a pin, and stick them on in rounds as thick as they can lye upon the said Cream, garnishing your Dish with them, and strow them over with the finest Sugar and serve them up.'

# GOOSEBERRY CREAM

Serves 4-6

This is a more modern version of Mrs. Cromwell's recipe.

**1 lb (450 g) gooseberries**
**3 tablespoons water**
**Sugar to taste**
**½ pint (300 ml/1¼ cups) cream**
**3 egg yolks**
**2 oz (50 g) butter**
**1 tablespoon orange-flower water**

Top and tail the gooseberries and wash them well.

Put into a saucepan with the water and cook gently until soft.

Pass the cooked fruit through a sieve.

Add sugar to taste.

Beat in the cream, the egg yolks, and the melted butter.

Add the orange-flower water.

Cook the mixture gently over a low heat until it is very thick, but do not allow to boil.

Spoon into a serving dish and leave to cool.

Alternatively, the gooseberry cream can be turned into a pastry case and baked in a moderately hot oven until set.

This tart may be eaten hot or cold.

Oven: 375°F/190°C  Gas Mark 5

# SUFFOLK LEMON SOLID

Serves 4

This set cream used to be very popular for tea, served with soft fruit.

**1 pint (600 ml/2½ cups) milk**
**2 lemons**
**6 oz (175 g) sugar**
**½ oz (15 g) powdered gelatine**

Put the milk, the grated rind from the lemons, the sugar, and the gelatine into a saucepan and heat gently until the sugar and gelatine have completely dissolved.

Add the juice from the lemons and stir until the milk separates and forms curds.

Pour the mixture into a basin.

Leave to cool and turn out when set.

# SUFFOLK SYLLABUB

**Grated rind of 1 lemon**
**4 oz (100 g) sugar**
**1 glass sherry**
**1 glass brandy**
**½ pint (300 ml/1¼ cups) double cream**

Mix together the lemon rind and sugar.

Pour over the sherry and brandy and leave until the sugar has dissolved.

Pour in the cream, stirring all the time.

Whisk until the mixture thickens.

Pour into individual  glasses and leave overnight in the refrigerator.

Serve the next day.

# GREENGAGE MOULD

Serves 4

**8 oz (225 g) greengages**
**2 oz (50 g) cornflour**
**1 pint (600 ml/2½ cups) milk**
**2 oz (50 g) sugar**

Stew the greengages until they are tender.

Remove the stones and pass the pulp through a sieve.

Mix the cornflour to a smooth cream with a little of the milk.

Add the sugar to the rest of the milk and bring to the boil, stirring so that the sugar dissolves.

Add the cornflour paste to the boiling milk, stirring well, and continue boiling until the milk thickens.

Add the greengage pulp and stir over the heat for a few more minutes.

Turn out into a serving dish and leave to go cold.

# BAKED CUSTARD

Serves 6

3 eggs
1½ oz (40 g) caster sugar
1½ pints (900ml/3¾ cups) milk
**Grated nutmeg**

Grease an ovenproof pie dish.

Beat the eggs and the sugar together.

Warm the milk and stir into the egg mixture.

Strain into the greased pie dish.

Sprinkle with grated nutmeg.

Stand the dish in a tray of warm water and bake slowly in a moderate oven for about 1 hour, or until the custard is set.

Oven: 350°F/180°C  Gas Mark 4

# FRUIT CAKE

4 oz (100 g) butter
4 oz (100 g) lard
8 oz (225 g) caster sugar
4 eggs
1½ lbs (675 g) plain flour
4 oz (100 g) glacé cherries
4 oz (100 g) crystallized ginger
4 oz (100 g) crushed pineapple (tinned)
4 oz (100 g) raisins
2 oz (50 g) chopped almonds
Juice of 1 lemon

Grate and line a large loose-bottomed cake tin.

Cream together the butter, lard and sugar, beating until white and fluffy.

Add the eggs separately, beating well after each addition.

Sift the flour and fold into the creamed mixture.

Chop the cherries and crystallized ginger, and add to the mixture with the pineapple, raisins, chopped almonds and lemon juice.

Turn into the cake tin and bake in a moderate oven for 2 hours.

Oven: 350°F/180°C Gas Mark 4

# SUFFOLK APPLE CAKE

Serves 6-8

8 oz (225 g) flour
1½ tablespoons baking powder
A pinch of salt
4 oz (100 g) beef dripping or lard
2 oz (50 g) sugar
8 oz (225 g) cooking apples
A little milk

Grease a baking sheet.

Sift the flour, baking powder and salt into a mixing basin.

Rub in the dripping or lard until the mixture resembles breadcrumbs.

Stir in the sugar.

Peel and core the apples and chop into small pieces.

Add to the other ingredients.

Add enough milk to make a firm dough.

Make the dough into a round, flat cake about ¼ inch (0.5 cm) thick.

Place the cake on the greased baking sheet and bake in a moderately hot oven for about 45 minutes, until well-risen and golden brown.

Eat hot, split open and buttered.

Oven: 375°F/190°C  Gas Mark 5

# OLD SIMNEL CAKE

This rich simnel cake was traditionally eaten on the fourth Sunday in Lent, Mothering Sunday.

½ oz (15 g) fresh yeast
A little milk to mix
2 lbs (900 g) plain flour
A pinch of salt
1 teaspoon bicarbonate of soda
12 oz (350 g) butter
1 lb (450 g) raisins
1 lb (450 g) currants
8 oz (225 g) cut mixed peel
8 oz (225 g) chopped almonds
8 oz (225 g) sugar
1 teaspoon ground cinnamon

Grease a loose-bottomed cake tin and line with greaseproof paper high enough to form a collar over the top, so that when the cake rises it will keep its shape.

Cream the yeast with a little sugar and some lukewarm milk.

Leave to rise.

Sift the flour, salt and bicarbonate of soda into a mixing basin.

Cut the butter into small pieces and rub into the flour.

Add the dried fruit, almonds, sugar and ground cinnamon.

Add the yeast mixture and knead thoroughly, adding enough extra milk to make a smooth dough.

Turn the cake mixture into the tin and bake in a cool oven for 1½-2 hours.

Oven: 300°F/150°C  Gas Mark 2

# NEWMARKET CAKE

12 oz (350 g) caster sugar
8 oz (225 g) butter
4 eggs, separated
12 oz (350 g) self-raising flour
3 oz (75 g) grated chocolate
3 heaped teaspoon instant coffee
¼ pint (150 ml/ ⅔ cup) water
3 oz (75 g) chopped almonds

Grease an 8 inch (20 cm) cake tin and line it with greaseproof paper.

Cream the sugar and butter together.

Beat in the egg yolks.

Sift the flour, and fold into the creamed mixture.

Add the grated chocolate, and the coffee mixed with the water.

Beat the egg whites until they stand in stiff peaks and fold into the mixture.

Add the finely chopped almonds.

Spoon the mixture into the cake tin and bake in a moderate oven for about 2 hours, or until the centre is firm to the touch.

Turn out and cool on a wire rack.

Oven: 325°F/160°C  Gas Mark 3

# SEED CAKE

When the wheat-sowing was completed the farmworkers would be treated to seed cake. The poet Tusser (1523-1580) wrote:

> "Wife, some time this weeke, if the wether hold cleere
> And end of wheat-sowing we make for this yeare.
> Remember you, therefore, though I do it not,
> The Seed-cake, the pasties and Furmentie-pot."

**3 eggs**
**2 teaspoons orange-flower water**
**8 oz (225 g) sugar**
**1 teaspoon caraway seeds**
**6 oz (175 g) plain flour**
**Grated rind of 1 lemon**

Grease an 8 inch (20 cm) cake tin.

Break the eggs into a bowl over a pan of boiling water.

Beat well until thick and creamy.

Add the orange-flower water, sugar and caraway seeds.

Whisk for 15 minutes.

Fold in the flour and lemon rind.

Turn into the cake tin and bake in a moderate oven for 1 hour.

Oven: 325°F/160°C  Gas Mark 3

# FOURSES CAKE

This traditional bread was served to harvesters in the afternoon, together with sugar beer. The name may be derived from the fact that the cake was marked into four sections, or because it was served at the four o'clock break.

**1 lb (450 g) plain flour**
**1 level teaspoon salt**
**1 level teaspoon mixed spice**
**4 oz (100 g) lard**
**½ oz (15 g) fresh yeast**
**1 teaspoon sugar**
**Approx ½ pint (300 ml/1¼ cups) warm water**
**4 oz (100 g) currants**

Sift the flour, salt and spice into a large mixing basin.

Cut the lard into small pieces and rub into the flour.

Cream the yeast with the sugar and a little warm water and add to the flour.

Add enough water to make an elastic dough.

Knead thoroughly.

Cover and leave in a warm place until the dough has doubled in size.

Knock the dough back and knead in the currants.

Shape into a large round and place on a greased baking sheet and leave to prove for a further 15 minutes.

Using the back of the knife mark into four sections.

Brush with milk to glaze and bake in a moderately hot oven for 45 minutes, until the bread is well risen and golden brown.

Oven: 400°F/200°C Gas Mark 6

# GOD'S KITCHEL CAKES

These cakes were given to godchildren, and were traditionally made during the Twelve Days of Christmas.

2 oz (50 g) butter
8 oz (225 g) currants
2 oz (50 g) cut mixed peel
2 oz (50 g) ground almonds
½ teaspoon cinnamon
½ teaspoon nutmeg
1 lb (450 g) puff pastry
Caster sugar

For the puff pastry:
8 oz (225 g) plain flour
6 oz (175 g) butter
Salt
Water to mix
For a richer pastry use equal amounts of butter to flour

To make the puff pastry:

Sift the flour.

Cut the butter into small pieces.

Add half the fat to the flour with a pinch of salt and cold water to make a dough.

Knead it quickly and roll until approximately ¾ inch (19 mm) thick.

Add the remaining butter.

Fold and roll again, dusting each time with a little flour.

To make the filling:

Soften the butter to mix it with the currants, mixed peel, ground almonds and spices.

Roll out half the pastry thinly to a square.

Spread the filling over the pastry.

Dampen the edges and cover with the other half of the pastry.

Press the edges together and seal.

Mark the pastry into 2 inch (5 cm) squares, but do not cut right through it.

Put onto a greased baking sheet and bake in a hot oven for about 25 minutes, until the pastry is well-risen and golden brown.

Sprinkle with caster sugar while still hot.

Divide into the marked squares.

Oven: 450°F/230°C  Gas Mark 8

# SUFFOLK BUNS

Makes 10-12

**1 lb (450 g) plain flour**
**1 oz (25 g) baking powder**
**A pinch of salt**
**6 oz (175 g) butter**
**6 oz (175 g) caster sugar**
**3 oz (75 g) currants**
**½ oz (15 g) caraway seeds**
**2 eggs**
**½ pint (300 ml/ 1¼ cups) milk**

Grease a baking sheet.

Sift the flour, baking powder and salt into a mixing basin.

Cut the butter into small pieces and rub into the flour.

Mix in the sugar, currants and caraway seeds.

Beat the eggs and stir them into the mixture.

Add enough milk to give a fairly stiff consistency.

Roll out the dough to 1 inch (2.5 cm) thick and cut into rounds.

Place buns on the greased baking sheet and brush the tops with milk.

Bake in a hot oven for 15-20 minutes until golden brown.

Oven: 425°F/220°C  Gas Mark 7

# BROTHERLY LOVE

**1 lb (450 g) plain flour**
**1 teaspoon salt**
**2 oz (50 g) lard**
**½ oz (15 g) fresh yeast**
**2 oz (50 g) caster sugar**
**½ pint (300 ml/1¼ cups) warm water**

Sift the flour and salt into a mixing basin.

Rub in half the lard.

Add the yeast creamed with a teaspoonful of the sugar and the warm water.

Mix to a smooth dough, kneading well.

Cover and leave in a warm place to rise until doubled in size.

Knock back the dough and roll out into a rectangle ½ inch (1 cm) thick.

Cut the rest of the lard into small flakes and dot these over the dough.

Sprinkle on the rest of the sugar.

Roll up to a sausage shape and place on a greased baking tray.

Leave in a warm place to prove for a further 15 minutes.

Bake in a hot oven for 30 minutes.

Oven: 425°F/220°C  Gas Mark 7

# SUFFOLK RUSKS

Makes 16

Traditionally, baking used to be done in brick ovens. Faggots or dry gorse would be burned inside the oven until it was heated up — this took about an hour. Then the fire was scraped out and the weekly joint, which would take about 2 hours to roast, was put in at the back. The bread dough was put in next, and Suffolk Rusks, which only took 10 minutes to bake, were put in at the front. These small yeast cakes were then dried in the oven after baking until they were brown and crisp, like rusks.

1 lb (450 g) plain flour
2 teaspoons salt
½ oz (15 g) fresh yeast
2 level teaspoons sugar
2 oz (50 g) lard
¼ pint (150 ml/⅔ cup) warm milk and water mixed
2 eggs

Sift the flour and salt into a mixing basin.

Cream the yeast with the sugar and a little of the warmed milk and water and add to the flour.

Melt the lard in the remaining warm liquid and add it with the beaten eggs to the mixing basin.

Knead lightly until you have a smooth dough.

Leave the dough in a warm place to rise until it has doubled in size.

Grease two baking sheets.

Knock the dough back, divide it into 16 equal-sized portions, and roll them out to 3 inch (7.5 cm) long rectangles.

Leave to prove for a further 10 minutes.

Bake in a hot oven for 10 minutes.

Remove the cakes from the oven and pull them in half lengthways.

Reduce the temperature of the oven.

Return the rusks to the oven for a further 15 minutes until they are brown and crisp.

Oven: 425°F/220°C  Gas Mark 7
Reduce to: 350°F/180°C  Gas Mark 4

# SUFFOLK RUSKS (another way)    Makes 10-12

Suffolk rusks can be made with self-raising flour if you don't want to use yeast. These rusks should be crisp and lightly browned, and not soggy in the middle. The stage at which you take them out of the oven the first time is crucial — they must have had time to rise and split slightly, but not be fully cooked. They are delicious served buttered or topped with cheese or other savouries.

**6 oz (175 g) self-raising flour**
**A pinch of salt**
**2 oz (50 g) lard**
**1 oz (25 g) margarine**
**1 egg, beaten**
**A little milk**

Grease a baking tray.

Sift the flour and salt into a mixing basin.

Rub in the fats so that the mixture resembles breadcrumbs.

Add the beaten egg and enough milk to make a soft dough.

Roll out the dough on a floured board to ½ inch (1 cm) thick and cut out into small rounds using a pastry cutter.

Place on the baking tray and bake in a moderately hot oven for 10 minutes, until the rusks have risen and there is a crack in the middle.

Remove from the oven and use two forks to split the rusks.

Reduce the temperature of the oven and continue baking the split rusks until they are crisp and brown.

Leave the rusks to cool.

Store in an airtight tin until required.

Oven: 400°F/200°C  Gas Mark 6
Reduce to: 350°F/180°C  Gas Mark 4

# SUFFOLK CAKES

Makes 12-16

**4 eggs, separated**
**8 oz (225 g) caster sugar**
**Grated rind of half a lemon**
**4 oz (100 g) softened butter**
**4 oz (100 g) plain flour**

Beat the whites of the eggs until they are stiff and stand in peaks.

Beat the yolks and stir into the whites.

Sift the sugar into the egg mixture.

Add the grated lemon rind.

Beat in the softened butter.

Sift in the flour and fold into the mixture.

Spoon the mixture into greased patty tins and bake in a moderately hot oven for 15-20 minutes, until the cakes are firm to the touch and light brown in colour.

Oven: 375°F/190°C  Gas Mark 5

# SUFFOLK FRUMENTY

Serves 6-8

Frumenty used to be eaten during the twelve days of Christmas — December 25th to January 5th. Some was placed on a plate outside the door at night for the 'Pharisees' (fairies) — which suggests that frumenty was made and eaten before England became Christian.

Frumenty makes an excellent breakfast food, providing plenty of roughage.

**8 oz (225 g) pearled wheat or barley**
**3 pints (1.75 litres/7½ cups) water**
**A pinch of salt**
**About 2 pints (1.15 litres/5 cups) milk**
**½ level teaspoon cinnamon**
**Honey to taste**
**1 oz (25 g) cornflour (optional)**

Put the grain into an ovenproof dish, cover with water and add a pinch of salt.

Cook in a slow oven for several hours until the grain has "creed" into a soft, jelly-like mass and absorbed all the water.

When required for use, put the creed wheat into a large saucepan and add double the quantity of milk, cinnamon, and honey to taste.

Boil for 10-15 minutes until thick and creamy.

If necessary, stir in the cornflour mixed with a little milk to thicken the frumenty.

Serve hot.

# DAMSON CHEESE

Fruit cheeses and butters were made when there was a glut of fruit because a large quantity makes only a small amount of finished preserve. The cheese is very rich and should not be served in large quantities. Small straight-sided jars, or old cups, make suitable moulds from which the fruit cheese can be turned out whole for serving. The cheese should be stored for at least a year for the flavours to develop. It can be eaten as a dessert, decorated with blanched almonds and served with whipped cream. Or it may be eaten with cold meats.

**3 lbs (1.5 kg) damsons**
**1 lb (450 g) preserving sugar to each 1 lb (450 g) pulp**

Put the washed damsons in a pan and cover with water.

Bring to the boil and simmer until the fruit is soft.

Rub the flesh through a sieve, leaving the skins and stones behind.

Measure the pulp and allow 1 lb (450 g) sugar to 1 lb (450 g) pulp.

Put the pulp and sugar in a pan and stir over a low heat until the sugar has dissolved.

Bring to the boil and simmer gently until a wooden spoon drawn across the bottom of the pan leaves a clear line.

Brush the insides of the moulds with olive oil so that the cheese will turn out easily.

Pour the cheese into the moulds.

Cover immediately with waxed paper discs, and when cool put on jam covers.

# GREENGAGE JAM   Makes about 5 lbs (2.25 kg)

**3 lbs (1.5 kg) greengages**
**3 lbs (1.5 kg) sugar**
**½ pint (300 ml/ 1¼ cups) water (very ripe fruit will
need less)**

Wash the greengages and remove the stalks.

Put into a large pan with water, and stew slowly until the
fruit is well broken down.

Add the sugar, and stir over a low heat until dissolved.

Bring to the boil and boil rapidly, removing the stones as they
rise to the surface.

After about 10 minutes test for setting point — spoon a little
jam onto a cold plate, and if setting point has been reached
the surface will set and will wrinkle when pushed with the
finger.

Skim the jam before spooning into warmed jars.

Cover the jars immediately.

82

# BLACKBERRY CORDIAL

A tablespoon of blackberry cordial taken in a glass of hot water at bedtime was a very popular remedy for the common cold.

**2 pints (1.15 litres/ 5 cups) ripe blackberries**
**1 pint (600 ml/ 2½ cups) white vinegar**
**1 lb (450 g) loaf sugar**
**8 oz (225 g) honey**

Put the blackberries into an earthenware or plastic jar.

Pour on the vinegar and leave to stand for a week.

Stir and press the berries each day to squeeze out the juice.

After a week strain the liquid into a saucepan.

Add the sugar and honey and bring the mixture to the boil, stirring all the time.

Boil for 5 minutes, then leave to cool.

When cool, pour the cordial into bottles with corks.

Store in a cool place.

# RHUBARB WINE

The abundant fruits of Suffolk have made home wine-making a favourite pastime.

Gather the quantity of rhubarb you require and cut it into small pieces.

For each 1 pint (600 ml/ 2½ cups) of rhubarb you will need 1 pint of water.

Put the rhubarb into a earthenware or plastic tub and pour on the water.

Leave to stand for two weeks, stirring and pressing the rhubarb each day to squeeze out the juice.

After two weeks strain off the liquid.

Measure 8 oz (225 g) sugar to each 1 pint (600 ml/ 2½ cups) liquid, and add this to the rhubarb juice.

Leave to stand for another week, skimming off the accumulated scum each morning.

Pour into clean bottles and cork.

Store in a cool place.

# SUGAR BEER

Sugar beer was served at harvest time with Fourses Cake. It will only keep for a couple of days.

**½ pint (300 ml/ 1¼ cups) hops**
**1 gallon (4.5 litres) water**
**Honey**
**1 tablespoon brewer's yeast**

Add the hops to the water and bring to the boil.

Simmer for 2 hours.

Add honey to sweeten, according to taste.

Spread the brewer's yeast on a piece of toast and float on top of the beer.

Cover with a cloth and leave overnight.

Next day skim off the froth before drinking.

# THE COUNTRY RECIPE SERIES

Available now @ £1.95 each

Cambridgeshire
Cornwall
Cumberland & Westmorland
Devon
Dorset
Hampshire
Kent
Lancashire
Leicestershire
Norfolk
Oxfordshire
Somerset
Suffolk
Sussex
Warwickshire
Yorkshire

-------------------------------------------------------------------------------

All these books are available at your local bookshop or newsagent, or can be ordered direct from the publisher. Just tick the titles you require and fill in the form below. Prices and availability subject to change without notice.

-------------------------------------------------------------------------------

Ravette Books Limited, 3 Glenside Estate, Star Road, Partridge Green, Horsham, West Sussex RH13 8RA.

Please send a cheque or postal order, and allow the following for postage and packing. UK 25p for one book and 10p for each additional book ordered.

Name.............................................................................................

Address.........................................................................................

.......................................................................................................

.......................................................................................................